# CONTENTS

# MAPS AROUND US

If you travel somewhere by car, or go for a long walk, you probably take a map with you. For centuries, people have used maps to find their way from one place to another. However, maps are not only used to get from A to B. They can also show information such as where earthquakes are likely to happen, or where rich and poor people live. Some maps mark political boundaries; others show the Earth's features, such as mountains, rivers and lakes. This book tells the story of maps from the earliest plans carved on stone to the latest computer-drawn charts. Making and studying maps is called cartography.

## SCALES AND SYMBOLS

The places, features and distances shown on a map have to be greatly reduced in size. So maps use a scale, for example on some maps one centimetre represents one kilometre. Map-makers use colours, shapes, lines and other symbols to display information. There are often grid lines running across a map, which help you to find landmarks easily. Most maps have a key, showing the scale, and explaining what the colours and symbols stand for.

## MAP PROJECTIONS

The surface of the Earth is curved, but most maps are flat. Map-makers have to distort the size, shape or position of countries in order to draw the Earth's surface on to a flat map. This is called a map projection. There are many different kinds of map projection. However, only a globe can show the surface of the whole Earth accurately.

*A modern globe*

## SIGNPOST

You might think you need hundreds of colours to shade in all the countries on a map of the world. In fact, you only need four or five. These can be arranged so that no two neighbouring countries are the same colour.

# FROM SEXTANT TO SONAR

## The story of maps and navigation

by Anita Ganeri

Evans Brothers
Limited

Published by Evans Brothers Limited
2A Portman Mansions
Chiltern Street
London W1M 1LE

First published 1998

Printed in Hong Kong by Wing King Tong Co. Ltd

**Acknowledgements**
**Editor:** Nicola Barber
**Design:** Neil Sayer
**Production:** Jenny Mulvanny
With thanks to Peter Barber, Deputy Map Librarian, British Library, who acted as consultant on this title.

British Library Cataloguing in Publication Data

Ganeri, Anita
  From sextant to sonar: the
  story of maps and navigation. - (Signs of the times)
  1.Cartography - Juvenile literature
  2.Cartography - History - Juvenile
  literature 3.Navigation - Juvenile literature
  4.Navigation - History - Juvenile literature
  I.Title
  526

ISBN 0237517450

**Acknowledgements**
The author and publishers would like to thank the following for permission to reproduce photographs:
Cover (top left) Science Museum/Science and Society Picture Library (top right) Adrienne Hart-Davis/Science Photo Library (centre) Earth Satellite Corporation/Science Photo Library (bottom left) Royal Geographical Society/Bridgeman Art Library
Back cover  Harriet Wynter Antiques/Bridgeman Art Library
Title page Ancient Art and Architecture page 6 Robert Harding Picture Library page 7 (top) British Library (middle) Philips Car Systems (bottom) Ancient Art and Architecture page 8 (left) Museum of Mankind (right) Nik Wheeler/Robert Harding Picture Library page 9 Gordon Langsbury/Bruce Coleman (bottom) Ancient Art and Architecture page 10 (left) Ancient Art and Architecture (right) Peter Clayton page 11 (left) Ancient Art and Architecture (right) e.t.archive page 12 (top) Simon Harris/Robert Harding Picture Library (bottom) British Library page 13 (left) e.t archive (right) British Library page 14 (left) Ancient Art and Architecture (right) Ancient Art and Architecture page 15 (top) British Library page 16 (left) Civicio Museo Storico Como/Robert Harding Picture Library (right) British Library page 17 (top) British Library (bottom) Mary Evans Picture Library page 18 (left) Galaxy Picture Library (right) e.t. archive page 19 (top) London Transport Museum (bottom) © British Crown copyright. Reproduced with the permission of the Controller of HMSO. page 20 (top) Ancient Art and Architecture (bottom) Dr Eckart Pott/Bruce Coleman Limited page 21 (top) Geoff Renner/Robert Harding Picture Library (bottom) Royal Geographical Society/Bridgeman Art Library page 22 (top) Science Museum/Science and Society Picture Library (bottom) John Bethell/Bridgeman Art Library page 23 (top left) Worshipful Company of Clockmakers' Collection/Bridgeman Art Library (top right) e.t. archive (bottom) David Parker/Science Photo Library page 24 (left) Private Collection/Bridgeman Art Library (right) Geco UK/Science Photo Library page 25 (top) Alison Wright/Robert Harding Picture Library (top inset) Royal Geographical Society (bottom left) Ordnance Survey (bottom left) British Library page 26 (top) Mary Evans/Explorer (bottom) Ancient Art and Architecture page 27 (top left) Institute of Oceanographic Sciences/Nerc/Science Photo Library (bottom left) BP/NRSC/Science Photo Library (right) ESA, EURIMAGE/Science Photo Library page 28 (top) Ancient Art and Architecture (bottom) Science Museum/Science and Society Picture Library page 29 Private Collection/Bridgeman Art Library

## MAPPING ABOVE AND BELOW

Many maps illustrate the surface of the Earth, but not all. Astronomers use maps that show the position of the stars in the sky, or the surface of the Moon. Geologists use maps of rocks under the ground to help them find oil or precious metals. Oceanographers use the latest technology to produce maps of the deep sea floor. Doctors study maps of the human body and brain, and maps showing how diseases have spread.

*A map of the Moon's surface, drawn by a German cartographer in 1837*

*An in-car navigation system. Information is displayed on a small screen.*

## IN-CAR CONTROL

Some modern cars have computerised navigation systems to help drivers find their way. Drivers feed information into the computer to tell it where they want to go. Then, on a small screen, the computer displays the quickest route (left). Some computers even have voices which tell drivers where to turn right or left, and which roads to avoid because of traffic jams.

## IN FACT...

An atlas is a collection of maps in a book. The name comes from the Ancient Greek myth about the giant, Atlas. According to legend, Atlas was condemned by the gods to carry the heavens on his shoulders (right). The first collection of maps in a book was published by a Belgian map-maker, Abraham Ortelius, in 1570. The word 'atlas' was first used in 1595, when another map-maker, Gerard Mercator, published a collection of maps with a picture of Atlas on the front page.

# BEFORE MAPS

Most of the world has now been mapped and charted. But this wasn't always the case. Before people had maps to guide them they relied on the Sun, stars and familiar landmarks to find their way about, or they simply asked the way from local people. Of course, their view of the world was very different from ours today. They had no satellites or aeroplanes to show them places far away. They guessed that there were distant, unknown lands, but they had no detailed knowledge of these places.

## IN FACT...

The oldest known plan of an inhabited place was carved on a rock face in northern Italy, 4,000 years ago. Pictures were used to show people, animals and houses. Other symbols – rectangles, circles and lines – may represent fields, wells and streams.

## STICKY GUIDES

The Polynesians were the first people to explore the vast Pacific Ocean, over 2,000 years ago. They had no charts or instruments to guide them. Yet they were skilled navigators and sailors who used the changing direction of the wind and waves to find land. Over the centuries, Polynesian sailors have continued to travel thousands of kilometres across the sea. Some of them made charts from palm sticks tied together with coconut thread. The sticks represented the sea, with tiny shells threaded on to show the islands.

*Outrigger canoes in the Pacific Ocean. The Polynesians used larger versions of canoes like these to explore the South Pacific.*

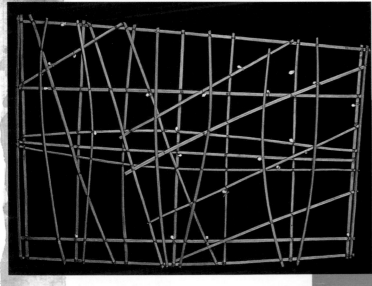

*A Polynesian stick map with tiny shells*

# SIGNPOST

Polynesian sailors sometimes followed the flight of migrating birds to help them find land. But how do birds find their way? Many birds fly thousands of kilometres to the same places, year after year. Some seem to be guided by the Sun, or by the Moon and stars if they fly by night. Some follow landmarks, such as mountains, deserts, waterfalls and rivers. Others may use the Earth's magnetic field to guide them.

*Each year, the Arctic tern makes an incredible journey of 40,000 kilometres from the Arctic to the Antarctic and back again.*

## SACRED LANDSCAPE

The Aborigine people of Australia believe that the world was created long ago, during the Dreamtime. This was when the spirits of their ancestors, in animal and human form, travelled across Australia shaping the hills, caves, lakes and waterholes. This means that, for the Aborigines, the landscape is sacred. The routes that the ancestors took are known as 'songlines'. Some are just a few kilometres, others several hundred kilometres long. Boys learn about the songlines in special ceremonies to mark the start of their adult life.

## HUNTING GROUNDS

Like the Aborigine people of Australia, many Native North Americans considered the land to be sacred. The traditional hunting grounds of the Pawnee people in central USA were bounded by five sacred sites, where the animals gathered. As long as the Pawnee stayed within these boundaries, good hunting was guaranteed.

*Aborigine artists painted their ancestor-animals on pieces of bark. These paintings acted like sacred maps to teach children about the Dreamtime.*

# EARLY MAPS

Early maps were drawn for many different reasons. Some maps were used to help people find their way. Others were needed for controlling and governing newly conquered lands. When kings and emperors went on journeys, they sometimes took their map-makers with them to fill in the gaps as they went along. However, many map-makers relied on information brought back by travellers, or on their knowledge of historical events, to put maps together.

## OLDEST MAP

The oldest known map of the world was drawn on a clay tablet in about 600 BC. It comes from Babylon (in present-day Iraq). The Earth is shown as a circle (see left), with Babylon at its centre and the Tigris and Euphrates rivers flowing through it (the two lines down the middle). The triangles are the 'Seven Islands' at the edge of the world where fabulous beasts were said to live. Around the world lies a vast ocean, called the 'Bitter River'.

*Babylonian world map*

## UNDERWORLD GUIDE

The Ancient Egyptians drew maps inside coffins to guide the dead person's soul. These maps showed routes through the Underworld to the next world, a happy, peaceful land somewhere to the far west. Two routes were given, one for travelling by day (shown in light colours) and one for travelling by night (shown in dark colours).

*An Ancient Egyptian map of the Underworld, inside a wooden coffin*

## THE GREEK WORLD

The Ancient Greeks believed that the world was made up of three continents, Europe, Asia and Africa, surrounded by a mighty river called Ocean. They also divided the world into five zones, based on climate. Around the middle, at the Equator, lay a baking hot zone where no one could live. To the far north and south lay two freezing zones, too cold to support life. Between these hot and cold zones lay two bands of pleasant, moderate weather. But no one could go from one to the other because they would not survive crossing the Equator.

## PTOLEMY OF ALEXANDRIA

The greatest geographer of ancient times was Ptolemy of Alexandria, in Egypt. In about AD 150, Ptolemy produced a guide to mapping the known world. His eight-volume *Geography* contained instructions on map-making and a list of 8,000 places, together with tables of latitude and longitude (see page 22).

## BREAKTHROUGH

In the 3rd century BC, Ancient Greek geographers in Alexandria, Egypt, made many amazing discoveries about the shape and size of the Earth. They were the first to state that the Earth was round. Most people thought it was flat. Eratosthenes, a brilliant scientist, calculated the Earth's circumference at 40,250 kilometres. He wasn't far off! In fact, the Earth measures 40,007 kilometres through the poles.

*The Alexandrian geographer, Ptolemy*

*A map of the world dating from 1486, based on Ptolemy's* Geography

## ROMAN ROUTES

The Romans used maps to govern their vast empire, and to make it easier to collect taxes. To impress visitors to Rome in the 1st century AD, a map of the world was put on display near the forum. The map showed the Roman Empire, with Rome at the centre.

## CHINESE CHARTS

Until they invented paper in about AD 105, the Chinese drew maps only on bamboo or silk. Two ancient silk maps have been found in Chinese tombs. They show rivers, mountains, settlements and a military garrison. Some maps were huge, made of as many as 80 rolls of silk. Like the Romans, the Chinese used maps to rule their empire. If the emperor knew the layout of his land, it was easier for his officials to govern it. There was an official map-maker in the emperor's court.

*The ruins of the forum in Rome. It was here that the Ancient Romans displayed their own version of a map of the world.*

*The Chinese continued to make silk maps until modern times. This map is printed on silk and dates from around 1800.*

## A MAP AND A MURDER

A map was used in an attempt to murder the first emperor of China, Shi Huang Di. In 227 BC, a man entered the emperor's palace carrying a precious silk map which he said contained important military secrets. When the emperor asked to see the map, the man unrolled it and pulled out a poisoned dagger hidden inside. Luckily the emperor managed to draw his sword and protect himself from his would-be assassin.

*Shi Huang Di, first emperor of China, survived several assassination attempts.*

## MONSTER MAPS

Many early map-makers used the writings of ancient authors and travellers' accounts as the basis for their maps. In the distant and unknown lands around the edges of their maps they often drew monsters such as dragons, giants and bizarre-looking people with horns or birds' wings. Many larger maps also showed men and women with dogs' heads, who barked instead of speaking!

*An early map of the world (a mappa mundi – see page 14), with a selection of strange monster-like people down the right-hand side, and dragons at the bottom*

## IN FACT...

A grid system of vertical and horizontal lines is drawn on to many maps to help pinpoint places more easily. The Greeks were the first to use grids, closely followed by the Chinese. Legend says that the Chinese grid was invented by a young woman who was weaving a military map for the emperor. The warp (lengthwise) and weft (crosswise) threads of the silk gave her the idea for the grid lines.

# MAPPING THE WORLD

In the Middle Ages, religion played a large part in European map-making. For Christian map-makers, the most important events happened in the Holy Land, so this region was the largest area on a map. However, in the 15th and 16th centuries, map-makers became more interested in the practical use of maps. At the same time, the voyages of explorers such as Christopher Columbus began to provide new information for European map-makers.

## MAPPA MUNDI

In the Middle Ages some Christian maps of the world, called *mappae mundi*, showed the Earth as a flat circle surrounded by a vast ocean. The holy city of Jerusalem usually lay at the centre. Other important places of pilgrimage, and pilgrimage routes, were also shown.

The 13th-century mappa mundi *from Hereford Cathedral, England*

## IN FACT...

On his famous voyage of discovery in 1492, Christopher Columbus thought he had reached Asia, not America. In fact he had miscalculated the size of the Earth. He based his calculations on those of Ptolemy, which made the Earth a quarter smaller than it actually was, but overestimated the size of Europe and Asia.

The Santa Maria, *the ship in which Columbus sailed to America*

*A Spanish portolan chart showing the Mediterranean and Atlantic coasts of Europe, and the coast of North Africa.*

## BREAKTHROUGH

In the 9th century AD, Arab map-makers came across copies of Ptolemy's *Geography* (see page 11) and translated it from Greek into Arabic. They used this translation as the basis for their studies. Few European map-makers had heard of Ptolemy's work until it was translated into Latin, the scholarly language of Europe, in the 1400s.

## PORTOLAN CHARTS

Medieval sea charts, called portolan charts, were probably used by sailors to navigate along the Mediterranean coast. A mesh of criss-crossed lines may have helped sailors to find their way from harbour to harbour. Drawn on sheepskins, portolan charts were first made in the 13th century in Italy and Spain. Their name means 'written sailing directions' in Italian.

## VINLAND FORGERY?

There is archaeological evidence to show that the Vikings reached America long before Christopher Columbus. In 1957, a map was discovered which seemed to back up this evidence. Drawn in the 15th century, it showed the voyage of Bishop Henricus of Greenland who sailed to Vinland, the Viking name for North America, in AD 1118. The Vinland Map caused great excitement. However, many experts are very doubtful about the map, and think that it could be a fake.

## MAKING PROJECTIONS

In 1569 a Dutch geographer called Gerard Mercator came up with a new way of showing the curved Earth on a flat map. Map-makers had been experimenting for centuries with different map projections (see page 6). Mercator's projection showed the Earth as a cylinder rolled out flat. The problem with this projection is that the further north or south you go, the more distorted the map gets. Some countries look bigger or smaller than they really are.

# EXPANDING THE FRONTIERS

From the 16th century onwards, map-makers became more concerned with the scientific accuracy of maps. New instruments and techniques helped to make maps more accurate. The demand for maps also grew as European settlers began to colonise the lands 'discovered' and claimed by explorers such as Christopher Columbus, Ferdinand Magellan and James Cook.

## MAPPING THE 'NEW WORLD'

The first surviving map to show the 'New World' of America was made by Christopher Columbus's pilot in 1500. Although Columbus is credited with the European 'discovery' of America, the new continent was named after his friend, the Italian navigator Amerigo Vespucci. Vespucci was Pilot Major of Spain, responsible for supervising and updating Spain's official maps and charts.

*A portrait of Christopher Columbus*

## BREAKTHROUGH

In 1529, the king of Spain's cartographer made the first map that showed the vast extent of the Pacific Ocean (below). He took his information from the survivors of Ferdinand Magellan's round-the world voyage. Magellan's historic expedition was the first to circle the globe. Five ships and 280 men set off from Spain in 1519. Three years later, one ship limped back home with 18 survivors on board. Magellan himself did not survive. He was killed in 1521.

*Magellan's route is shown by a blue line on this map.*

## UNKNOWN LANDS

Ptolemy's early maps showed a great southern landmass called *Terra Australis Incognito*, or 'Unknown Southern Land'. For centuries, extraordinary stories were told of this strange place where the rain fell upwards and people had feet higher than their heads! It was not until the 18th century that the region was mapped by Europeans. This task was undertaken mainly by Captain James Cook (see page 23), an English navigator and map-maker. He made three voyages to Australia, New Zealand, and into Antarctic waters. He used his new-found knowledge to draw up the first modern map of the Pacific Ocean.

*This map shows the USA from the Mississippi River to the Pacific Ocean. It was drawn up from information collected by William Clark and published in 1814.*

## ACROSS AMERICA

In 1804 the president of the USA, Thomas Jefferson, sent Meriwether Lewis and William Clark to explore western America and find a route to the Pacific coast. Travelling by land and river, Lewis and Clark's journey took two years to complete. Both men kept detailed notes of everything they saw. They got information from the local Native Americans who drew maps for them on animal hides, or on the ground. This information was transferred on to a master map by Clark. Clark's map was later used by many other American map-makers.

## IN FACT...

In the 19th and 20th centuries, many explorers were driven on by the wish to be the first to reach some of the world's wildest places. In 1911 the Norwegian explorer, Roald Amundsen, was the first to reach the South Pole. From the information gathered on this and other expeditions, much of Antarctica was mapped for the first time. This work still continues today.

*Amundsen and his companions raise the Norwegian flag at the South Pole.*

# FROM STARS TO STATIONS

While many cartographers were busy mapping the surface of the Earth, some map-makers turned their attention to other subjects. There are specialist maps showing the stars in the night sky, the weather, the development of a disease, and even some maps that don't quite tell the truth!

## SEEING STARS

The only way to draw an accurate map of the whole sky is to show it on the inside of a sphere, just as a globe shows the Earth on the outside of a sphere. This is what happens in a planetarium, when a picture of the stars is projected on to the spherical roof of a special theatre. However, star maps on paper flatten out the sky just as the Earth is flattened by using a particular projection (see page 6). One of the earliest known star maps was made by the Chinese in AD 310.

## MILITARY MAPS

Since Roman times, maps have been used for planning military campaigns and strategy. They have also been used to mislead the enemy. Some maps are sometimes deliberately falsified in case they fall into enemy hands during a war. Others leave out vital information that could be helpful to a potential enemy.

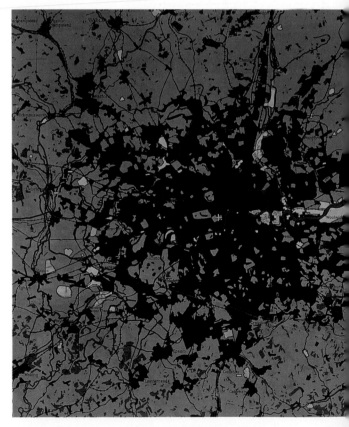

This German World War II map was used by pilots on bombing raids over London.

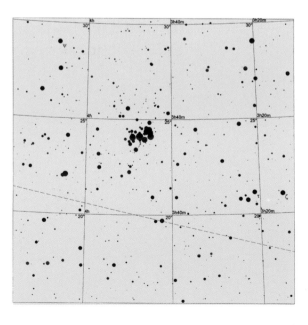

A modern star map showing part of the Pleiades cluster

18

Most maps show places correctly positioned in relation to each other. However, on some maps this does not matter. It is more important to show how places are linked. These are called topological maps. One famous example is the map of the London Underground. It shows how the stations and lines are connected but does not give details of every twist in the track nor the correct distances between them.

*One of the most famous examples of a topological map is the London Underground map, designed by Henry Beck in 1933.*

## CHOLERA MAPS

In 1855, Dr John Snow, Queen Victoria's doctor, used a technique called 'thematic mapping' to find the cause of an outbreak of a disease called cholera. Cholera is often spread through dirty water. On a map of central London, Dr Snow drew a dot to represent each person who had died of cholera that year. Most of the dots appeared around a water pump in Soho – the source of the infected water. The pump was quickly closed down.

## IN FACT...

Tactile maps are specially designed for blind people. Features are shown by raised dots which are felt with the fingers. The maps also give useful information, such as the position of kerbs, lamp-posts and other possible obstacles.

## WEATHER MAPS

Every day you can find out what the weather is going to be like by looking at weather maps in the newspapers or on the television. All over the world, weather stations collect data which is translated into maps and forecasts. Satellites orbiting the Earth show weather patterns, such as clouds and storms, which cannot be seen from the ground. The earliest weather maps were made in the USA in the 1840s.

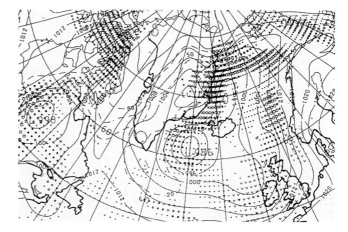

*Part of a weather map showing high-pressure and low-pressure areas over the Atlantic Ocean*

# NAVIGATION KNOW-HOW

Pinpointing your position on the Earth's surface and plotting a course from A to B is called navigation. The earliest navigators used the movements of the Sun, Moon, stars and planets, and the changing direction of the winds and waves to guide them. Others followed familiar landmarks or the flight patterns of birds. But the more people travelled, the more important it was to have accurate methods for finding the way.

## AROUND AFRICA

The Phoenicians were travelling and trading along the coast of the Mediterranean Sea about 3,000 years ago. They were the greatest sailors and navigators of their time. In about 600 BC, Phoenician explorers became the first to sail around Africa. It was a gruelling round trip of 25,000 kilometres which took three years to complete.

*A Phoenician trading ship from the 1st century BC*

## SIGNPOST

In about 310 BC the Greek explorer, Pytheas, set off on a daring six-year voyage across the north Atlantic. He sailed around Britain and then journeyed northwards to the Arctic, where he found himself surrounded by 'seas of ice'. Unfortunately, no one believed him! It wasn't until the 1st century AD that map-makers began to take his observations seriously.

*Pytheas's 'seas of ice' in the Arctic Ocean*

## BREAKTHROUGH

The basic tools of modern navigation are a compass and a chart. The first magnetic compass was used in China, in the 11th century. It was made from an iron needle which floated in a bowl of water. Left to swing freely, a magnetic needle will usually point roughly north-south along the Earth's magnetic field. This shows you where north is, and allows you to find your position on the Earth's surface.

## TRAVELLER OF ISLAM

Between 1325 and 1353 the great Arab explorer, Ibn Battuta, travelled over 120,000 kilometres. He journeyed across the Sahara, to the Middle East, India, Mongolia and China. He never took the same route twice, despite having no maps to guide him. On his return, he devoted himself to writing an account of his travels, a vital source of information for future historians and explorers.

## FINDING NORTH

A compass needle points towards magnetic north. This is different from true north which is marked by the North Pole. True north always stays in the same place, but magnetic north gradually moves over the years.

*A ship's compass, made in France and used by David Livingstone on his first expedition up the Zambezi River in Africa (1853-6)*

## IN FACT...

The first lighthouse was built in about 300 BC off Alexandria, Egypt. Its white marble tower stood 122 metres high, taller than the tallest modern lighthouse. Light from a wood fire in the top of the lighthouse was projected by mirrors to ships out at sea.

## USING A SEXTANT

A sextant is used to measure the angle between the horizon and the Sun in order to calculate latitude. The first accurate sextant was made in the 18th century. It is still a basic tool of navigation, used on land and at sea.

## SIGNPOST

You can plot the position of any place on Earth by its latitude and longitude. Both are measured in degrees. Latitude shows how far north or south of the Equator a place is. Longitude shows how far west or east of the Greenwich Meridian a place is. The Greenwich Meridian is an imaginary line running through Greenwich Observatory, London. It marks 0° longitude.

*An early sextant, made at the beginning of the 19th century*

*Greenwich Observatory in London*

## HARRISON'S SEA CLOCK

For centuries, measuring longitude accurately at sea was almost impossible. Many ships were wrecked because sailors were never quite sure where they were. This was because navigators needed to compare time to calculate longitude, but there were no accurate clocks suitable for use on board a ship (the pendulum clocks of the time were affected by the movement of the waves). In 1714, the British Parliament announced a £20,000 prize (about £800,000 in today's money) for the first person to make an accurate ship's clock. It was won by an English clock-maker called John Harrison, who invented an accurate clock known as a marine chronometer.

*The fifth version of Harrison's marine chronometer. Captain Cook took a copy of version four, a pocket-sized model, on his second voyage.*

## SIGNPOST

On his second voyage to the South Pacific in 1772-5, Captain Cook took one of Harrison's new marine chronometers with him. Without this 'trusty guide', Cook's accurate mapping of parts of the coastlines of Australia and New Zealand would have been impossible.

*Captain James Cook*

## ELECTRONIC NAVIGATION

The Global Positioning System (GPS) allows people on land, sea or in the air to find their position in any weather to within 50 metres. The GPS is made up of dozens of satellites that orbit the Earth. The satellites broadcast their exact position and the time. This information can be picked up by a small computer in your car or boat. The computer works out how long the signals take to reach it and tells you your location.

*This driver is using a portable satellite navigation receiver to check her exact position with the Global Positioning System.*

# SURVEYING AND MAP-MAKING

Surveyors measure the landscape and collect information about its landmarks and features. This information can then be used to create maps. Today, photographs from aircraft and satellites have revolutionised surveying, allowing ever more accurate measurements and maps to be made.

## EGYPTIAN SURVEYS

The Ancient Egyptians used their surveying skills for marking the boundaries of farmers' fields. The size of the fields was important because it determined how much tax the pharaoh (king) could demand from each farmer.

### IN FACT...

Egyptian and Roman surveyors used a number of surveying tools for measuring angles, including knotted ropes and gromas. A groma was made from two crossed sticks which were set at right angles to each other. Stones were hung from the four ends. A surveyor held the groma up, and worked out angles by measuring distant objects against the stones.

*Ancient Egyptian surveyors used knotted ropes to measure out their fields.*

## THEODOLITES

A theodolite measures angles. It is used by surveyors to find the height and position of an unknown point in relation to a known point. The earliest theodolite was made by the Greek scientist, Hero of Alexandria, in about AD 100. In the early 17th century, a telescope was added to make it easier to find distant reference points. Modern theodolites also have a built-in spirit level. They are used today to mark out building sites and the routes of new roads.

*Surveyors using a modern theodolite*

# SIGNPOST

Between 1800 and 1870 the whole of India was surveyed, using a series of gigantic triangles to measure vast areas of land. It was an amazing feat. The surveyors used 30-metre-long steel chains supported on tripods, and an enormous theodolite made of brass, glass and gun metal which weighed half a tonne. The heavy equipment and huge distances were not the only problems. The surveyors were also terrorised by tigers and laid low by diseases such as malaria and dysentery.

*Sir George Everest (right) and the Himalayan mountain named after him (above), the highest in the world. Everest was the driving force behind the Great Survey of India from 1821 until he retired in 1843.*

*Part of a modern Ordnance Survey map, and (inset) a cover from a 1930s one-inch-to-the-mile OS map*

© Crown Copyright Reserved

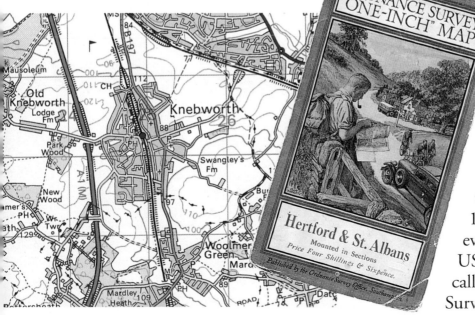

## ORDNANCE SURVEY

The Ordnance Survey (OS) was founded in 1791 to survey and map the whole of Britain. It was originally part of the army and the surveying was carried out by soldiers. The first OS maps (at a scale of one inch to a mile) were published in 1801. Today, OS maps cover every part of Britain. In the USA a similar organisation called the US Geological Survey was set up in 1879.

## MAP-MAKERS

Until the invention of printing, and for many centuries afterwards, maps were drawn and coloured by hand. Maps became works of art and many great artists, such as Leonardo da Vinci, Albrecht Dürer and Hans Holbein, tried their hand at cartography. From the 14th to the 16th centuries, Italy, Portugal and Spain were the centres of map-making. By the 17th century, cartographers in Belgium and the Netherlands had become famous for their map-making skills.

*A map of Africa, made in 1610 by cartographers in the Netherlands*

## IN FACT...

The rulers of Spain and Portugal in the 15th and 16th centuries tried hard to keep their latest 'discoveries' a secret. This was because they did not want sailors from rival countries to know about their new eastern trade routes. Many attempts were made to steal charts showing these routes. In 1502, an Italian spy set himself up as a Lisbon horse-dealer and managed to smuggle a copy of a chart out of Portugal. He would have been put to death if he had been caught.

*The port of Lisbon in the 16th century*

## FIRST PRINTED MAP

The earliest known printed map was made in China, in about AD 1155. It shows part of western China, bounded by the Great Wall. Printing was invented in China in the 8th century AD. When printing reached Europe in the 15th century, there was a great surge in map-making. Maps could now be made more cheaply and in larger numbers.

## COMPUTER CARTOGRAPHY

Today, many maps are drawn by computer. Information is fed into the computer. This data is then sorted, stored and arranged for mapping. A device called a plotter is linked to the computer. It uses the information in the computer to draw maps on paper or photographic film. Some plotters use pen and ink, others use laser beams.

## SEA FLOOR SONAR

Until very recently, no one knew what the ocean bed looked like. Then, in 1978, the *Seasat-A* satellite was launched to study the world's oceans. It orbited 800 kilometres above the Earth and built up a picture of the ocean floor, showing mountains and valleys, just as on land. Scientists also use sonar, or sound, to map the sea floor. This works by sending beeps of sound from an instrument towed above the sea bed. The sound bounces back off the sea bed as an echo. These signals are fed into a computer and used to build up a map.

*Launching GLORIA, an underwater sonar device used to build up a picture of the features of the deep-sea floor.*

# BREAKTHROUGH

Aerial photography is a very important technique in modern map-making. But it only became possible after the invention of powered flight in 1903. Today, satellites are also used to photograph the Earth. They take hundreds of pictures which are pieced together to make a map. Satellite photographs can show amazing detail, such as vegetation or areas of pollution. They can also reveal parts of the world never seen before, such as the shape of the land under the Antarctic ice.

*This satellite photograph shows crop patterns in fields in northern Germany.*

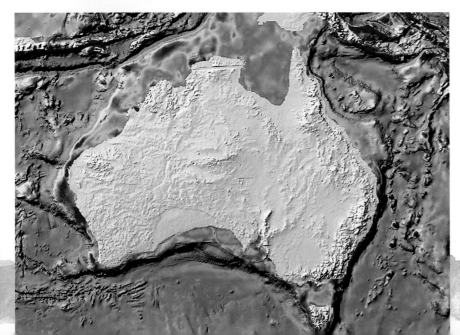

*A map of the sea floor around Australia, using information from the Seasat satellite. Different colours show the different depths of water. The shallowest water is red, the deepest is blue.*

# TIME TAPE

**BC**

— *c.* 2000  The oldest known plan of an inhabitated place is carved in Italy
— *c.* 1000-500 The Polynesians explore the Pacific Ocean
— *c.* 500  The oldest known world map is drawn in Babylon
— *c.* 310  Pytheas, Greek explorer, sails to the Arctic
— *c.* 240  Eratosthenes, Greek scientist, calculates the size of the Earth
— *c.* 190-120  Hipparchus, Greek scientist, first uses latitude and longitude

**AD**

— *c.* 105  The Chinese invent paper
— *c.* 150  Ptolemy publishes the *Geography*
— 310  First star maps made in China
— 1000-1100 Magnetic compasses used in China
— *c.* 1155  First printed map made in China
— 1200s  First portolan charts drawn
— 1280s  The Hereford *Mappa Mundi* is drawn
— 1304-77  Life of Ibn Battuta, Arab explorer
— 1451-1506  Life of Christopher Columbus
— 1519-21  Ferdinand Magellan leads the first expedition to sail around the world
— 1569  Famous map projection devised by Gerard Mercator
— 1570  First atlas made by Abraham Ortelius
— 1693-1776  Life of John Harrison, inventor of the marine chronometer
— *c.* 1758  First accurate sextant made
— 1768-76  Captain Cook explores and maps Australia and New Zealand
— 1791  Founding of Britain's Ordnance Survey (OS)
— 1800-70  Great Trigonometrical Survey of India
— 1804-6  Lewis and Clark cross the USA
— 1840s  First weather maps made in the USA
— 1879  Founding of the US Geological Society
— 1978  *Seasat-A* satellite begins to map the oceans
— 1990s  Cartographers use lastest computer and GPS technology

# GLOSSARY

**Cartographer** Someone who draws, plans and studies maps.

**Cartography** The making and studying of maps.

**Chronometer** An accurate, clock-like instrument, used for measuring time at sea. This information can then be used to calculate a ship's longitude.

**Compass** An instrument used in navigation. It shows you where north is and allows you to find your position in relation to north.

**Contour lines** Lines drawn on a map to join places which are the same height above sea level.

**Greenwich Meridian** An imaginary line which runs through Greenwich, London, and marks the line of 0° longitude.

**Groma** An ancient surveying tool used by the Ancient Egyptians and Romans for angles.

**Latitude** The measure of how far a place is to the north or south of the Equator.

**Longitude** The measure of how far a place is to the east or west of the Greenwich Meridian.

*Mappa mundi* A medieval map of the world. It showed the Christian view of the world, with the holy city of Jerusalem in the centre.

**Navigation** Finding your position on the Earth's surface, and plotting a course between A and B.

**Navigator** Someone in charge of, or skilled in, navigation.

**Portolan chart** A medieval sea chart from Italy or Spain, drawn on sheepskin. For their time, portolan charts were remarkably accurate.

**Projection** A way of showing the curved surface of the Earth on a flat map.

**Satellite** A man-made object launched from and orbiting the Earth. Satellites are used for surveying, navigation and communication.

**Scale** The sizes of and distances between objects on a map, compared to actual sizes and distances.

**Sextant** An instrument used in navigation. It is used to calculate latitude, by measuring the angle between the horizon and the Sun.

**Sonar** Short for 'sound navigation ranging'. Sonar instruments use sound to map the sea floor. Beeps of sound bounce off objects and send back echoes. These are fed into a computer to build up a picture of the area.

**Surveyor** A person who collects information about the land by measuring its size and shape. This information can be used to draw up maps.

**Theodolite** A surveying instrument used to measure horizontal and vertical angles.

**Topological map** A map showing how places are linked together, such as the stations in a railway network, without showing their correct positions or the correct distances between them.

# INDEX